# Old Shawlands and Newlands

## By Sandra Malcolm

Car 680 (Service 25) on Pollokshaws Road, at the junction with Titwood Road, as it approaches Shawlands from the city in 1928. This Standard tram came into service in December 1923 and was scrapped in October 1958. It originally worked out of Newlands Depot before moving to Langside in 1935. The land for Queen's Park was acquired in 1857 and was designed by Sir Joseph Paxton. The park was named after Mary, Queen of Scots, who lost the Battle of Langside in 1568. The land was originally owned by the Maxwells of Nether Pollok, but by the late 17th century the western end had been sold off to the Crawford family to form Camphill Farm. In 1799 Robert Thomson, a Glasgow manufacturer, bought the land and built Camphill House. His son bought Pathhead Farm, part of the lands of Langside, from the Maxwells in 1834; in 1857 the whole area was sold to Glasgow Corporation for £30,000.

Text © Sandra Malcolm, 2017.
First published in the United Kingdom, 2017,
by Stenlake Publishing Ltd.
Telephone: 01290 551122
www.stenlake.co.uk

ISBN 9781840337648

To the new 'Southsiders' – Rosa and Asha.

*Printed by*
P2D Books, 1 Newlands Rd,
Westoning, Bedford, MK45 5LD

**The publishers regret that they cannot supply copies of any pictures featured in this book.**

## Further Reading

R.V.J. Butt, *The Directory of Railway Stations* (1995)
Jack Gibson, *Pollokshaws: A Brief History* (1990)
Glasgow City Council, *Langside Heritage Trail*
Andrew Jeffrey, *This Time of Crisis* (1993)
Jack Kernahan, *The Cathcart Circle* (1980)
Aileen Smart, *Villages of Glasgow Volume 2* (1996)
Ian G. Stewart, *The Glasgow Tramcar* (1994)
Williamson, Riches & Higgs, *The Buildings of Scotland: Glasgow* (1990)

*Left*: Coronation Car 1215 (Service 8) on Kilmarnock Road, passing Millwood Street in September 1958. Brought in to service in October 1938, it was withdrawn in November 1961 having worked from the Langside Depot in Battlefield throughout its working life. Just out of sight to the left of the picture was the Cameo Ballroom. The Cameo was one of many ballrooms in Glasgow, the first being opened in Bath Street in 1905. By the 1920s Glasgow had more ballrooms than any other city in the UK. The dancing pastime remained popular for many decades. In 1968 the Cameo was advertising ballroom and lounge dancing with two bands for 7/6d. In 1973 bookings were being taken for a Christmas Dinner Dance for £1.50 and a Hogmanay Dance for £2. In 1960 Sir Alexander King, an astute businessman and cinema manager, owned the Cameo. He also owned the Elephant Cinema on Kilmarnock Road. King sold the land on which the cinema was built to the Murrayfield Real Estate Company Ltd who wished to build the Shawlands Arcade (the cost of which was to be around £200,000). He also proposed to build a two-storey tearoom as part of the Cameo but this did not come to fruition. You can still see the Cameo building at 52–54 Kilmarnock Road.

Cunarder 1314 (Service 14) on Pollokshaws Road beside what is now Shawlands Primary School. The first Cunarders came into service in 1948 and most of them were in service by 1950. Tram 1314 came into service in December 1949 and was scrapped in November 1962. The gardens at the right of the picture belonged to villas that were demolished in the 1960s when the Shawlands Arcade was developed.

Taken in May 1959 on Pollokshaws Road at Shawlands Cross, this photograph shows tramcar 812, a round Dash Standard which was brought into service in July 1900. Instead of being scrapped, this tram is preserved in the National Tramway Museum at Crich in Derbyshire. It was originally built as an open top tram, but in 1910 it was given a top cover with open balconies. In 1912 platform vestibules were added.

Car 1017, seen here in 1954 as it passes along Kilmarnock Road at the junction with Corrour Road and Newlandsfield Road. On 1 August 1923 Glasgow Corporation bought over Paisley District Tramways and in doing so increased the city's fleet by 73 'caurs'. Many of the Paisley trams were not in good enough condition to be used by Glasgow and so some of the trams were converted to single decker cars for a new service between Clydebank and Yoker. These cars were the first to be fitted with English Electric DK controllers and 'run-back' brakes as this service was so hilly. The single deckers were very suitable for driver training and car 1017 was specially converted to be a permanent Motor School Car. It was fitted with wooden transverse seating to allow 18 trainees to learn their skills and most of the bulkheads were removed so that all the trainee motormen had a clear view of what was going on. In this picture a sign on the side window can be seen that says 'School Car'. Car 1017 was withdrawn from service in August 1960. The tram directly behind is an ex-Liverpool 'Green Goddess'.

Car 1327 (service 8) on Pollokshaws Road at the crossroads approaching Shawlands Cross, 1958. On the right is Queen's Park. This Mark II Coronation or 'Cunarder' came into service on 31 March 1950 and was scrapped in August 1962. These trams provided seating for 70 passengers, at the expense of very little space between the seats. There were three steps to the platform – a design that did not find favour with many passengers as it made it difficult to get on or off. The letters HHS on the registration plate of the car on the left shows that the car was registered in Renfrewshire. The HHS codes were used from May 1954. The tenement on the left with the dome is Camphill Gate, built between 1905 and 1906. It has a flat roof, fenced off with an iron balustrade, which could be used as a drying green. The architect John Nisbet designed these tenements to be Glasgow's first fireproof building by installing a fireproof roof and walls throughout the building.

Shawlands Cross is dominated by two roads – Kilmarnock Road (on the left) and Pollokshaws Road (on the right). Kilmarnock Road is the main historic road between Glasgow and Irvine. Old maps suggest that Pollokshaws Road is aligned with the driveway to Pollok House and that perhaps both roads were intended to join. Mossside Road (at the far right of the picture) was originally a road leading to an orchard and a few houses. Most of the buildings in the picture were built from the mid-19th century to the early 20th century. The building at the gushet, known as Crossmyloof Mansions, was built *c.*1890. Its exterior walls have metal fixtures called 'rosettes' and these carried the electric cables that powered the trams. At the top of the building is an impressive balustrade parapet. Crossmyloof Mansions was made a category B listed building in 1992.

On the far left of the picture, behind Crossmyloof Mansions, is the Elephant Cinema. It was easy to spot as it had a large model elephant mounted over the entrance. The cinema was built by A.E. Pickard in 1927. He installed special 'lover's neuk' seats which were without centre armrests and did not have a view of the screen! The building was unusual in that it incorporated a car park. Pickard's own name for the cinema was 'White Elephant' and it changed its name to 'Elephant' in 1934 when it was sold to Alexander B. King. In the 1950s a Cinemascope screen was installed, along with a restaurant and dance hall. The cinema was sold in April 1960 to the Murrayfield Real Estate Company to allow for the redevelopment of Shawlands as a modern shopping centre with a supermarket.

Just behind the street lighting pole in the centre of the picture is an original police signal box. One of the first police telephone lines in the UK was manufactured for the City of Glasgow Police in 1880. Telephone lines linked Glasgow's western and central police stations. By 1889 all police and fire stations in Glasgow were linked by telephone. However, the authorities felt that the city needed better communications for their constables on the beat. The first signal box of the type seen here was a cast-iron structure, painted red and made by Macfarlane & Co's Saracen Foundry, and patented by a fireman, Charles Eggar. The light on the top of the box lit up when the station wished to communicate with a police officer on the street. He had to insert a 'constable' key to open the box. Fourteen boxes like this were erected in 1891 around the city at a cost of £500. It is likely that the box here was one of the first. By 1914 Glasgow had 56 of them.

When this photograph was taken in 1951, the police box seen here at Shawlands Cross was painted red: Scottish police boxes were not painted blue until the 1960s. In 1931 Percy Sillitoe was appointed Chief Constable of Glasgow and it was he who introduced the new kiosk design police boxes. By 1938 there were 323 police boxes on Glasgow streets. This may have contributed towards Sillitoe's success in breaking up the Glasgow razor gangs of the 1930s. The new boxes allowed members of the public to access the telephones for emergency situations.

At the left of the picture is the building that housed the Trustee (formerly Glasgow) Saving Bank. The Glasgow Savings Bank had its headquarters in Ingram Street. Founded in 1836, it was the largest bank of its type in the UK. It amalgamated with the West of Scotland Trustee Savings Bank in 1974 and TSB Scotland in 1983, merging once more with Lloyd's Bank in 1995. Designed by Neil Campbell Duff, the building here was built in Renaissance style with sculptured panels, friezes and tympana; it opened in 1906. The shelter on the right served bus and tram passengers alike, although apparently the Corporation staff did not like making use of it in this photograph!

The church on the left was originally a United Free church, built between 1900 and 1903 by Glasgow-based architects Miller and Black. Presentation drawings of the church were displayed at the annual exhibition of the Royal Glasgow Institute of Fine Arts in 1901. The hall for the church was built in 1898, designed in the Arts and Crafts style by John Hamilton. Following the United Free Church's merger with the Church of Scotland in 1929, the building became Shawlands Church of Scotland. In 1906–07 Glasgow Corporation paid £152/6/0 for a new public convenience at Shawlands Cross, the railings of which can be seen in the centre of the photograph. The children carrying briefcases were most likely going to Shawlands Secondary School in Moss-side Road.

At the right of the picture there is a sign for Pyramids Billiards. Originally the hall, the entrance to which is between two shop fronts, was Shawlands Picture House. This cinema was owned by the ABC and opened in 1914. Films were projected onto a white painted wall and the seating would have been basic wooden chairs. When it opened, most of the films would only have been ten to fifteen minutes in length. The cinema closed in 1930. Behind Pollokshaws Road, in Baker Street and virtually at the back of the Shawlands Picture House, was Camphill Picture House, which opened in 1911 with 820 seats. When it was taken over by John Maxwell's Scottish Cinema and Variety Theatres chain in 1929, it was enlarged to hold 1,200 customers but it closed in April 1931 after a disastrous fire.

The Commercial Bank of Scotland at 1098 Pollokshaws Road sat right beside the Bank of Scotland at No. 1096. The Commercial Bank of Scotland was established in 1810 in Edinburgh. It was begun principally to facilitate commercial, industrial and agricultural businesses. It issued its own banknotes and by 1815 had fourteen branches spread over the country. By 1860 it had become the second largest network of Scottish banks, with 56 branches and by 1920 it had 240 branches. In 1959 it merged with the National Bank of Scotland and became known as the National Commercial Bank of Scotland. At that point it had assets of £300 million. In 1969 it merged with the Royal Bank of Scotland.

This building stood where the Co-operative building now stands at 1078 Pollokshaws Road. A variety of services were offered by the traders based here: Best Household Coal Supplies, Hairdresser and Perfumer, William Muir Slater, William Allan Contractor, Victoria Laundry and William Thomson Boot and Shoemaker. Coal was supplied in bags or wagons and orders were promptly attended to, according to the advertising hoardings. Ladies shoes were soled and heeled for 1/6d. Gents shoes were slightly more expensive at 2/6d. Shaving cost 2d and hair cutting 4d.

All the buildings in these photographs have been demolished, but they used to be at 1066 Pollokshaws Road. The blacksmith's was variously called Crossmyloof Forge, Shawlands Smiddy and Hugh Galt Horseshoeing Forge and General Smith. Apart from shoeing horses, other services were offered, such as locks picked, keys cut and grates cut and repaired. To the left of the smith's was a cobbler advertising prices to have boots soled and heeled. On the other side is an advertising hoarding for 'The World's Way', a 1915 'anthology of the literature of social protest' edited by the American writer Upton Sinclair.

This is Mackie's Dairy, probably situated in Pollokshaws Road. It is likely that the milk would have come from Newlands Farm, which was situated where Newlands Road crosses St Bride's Road. The advertisement board at the side is promoting 'Cheap' railway excursions to London – 3rd class, 2/6d.

Seen here in 1951, Ross's Dairies at 1054 Pollokshaws Road was part of a chain of dairies and milk bars across Scotland. Scottish milk was promoted as the ideal drink in the 1930s – ironic really as Ross's tearooms had a smoking room for patrons. Interestingly, the growth of dairies in Scotland led to a boom in the tile manufacturing industry, as tiles gave the impression of a clean hygienic environment and were therefore in great demand for the shops. Bayne and Duckett's was founded by William Duckett and Christopher Bayne in 1858. The business provided for a demand for a greater variety of footwear by using commercial travellers and then opening branch shops. A limited company was formed in 1936, by which time there were 35 shops in Scotland and England. In 1928, when their new warehouse was opened at the corner of Brunswick Street and Wilson Street in Glasgow, their souvenir brochure stated, 'There is no doubt that the increased prosperity of the shoe trade dates from the advent of the short skirt …'. Despite this, there were no female directors or managers.

None of these buildings survive in Pollokshaws Road. All were demolished when tenement building began as the city expanded.

James McAllister had his slater and plastering business at 1106 Pollokshaws Road roughly between 1898 and 1910. It is believed that the property was originally used by a weaver; the villages of Strathbungo and Crossmyloof were mostly populated by weavers who worked in Pollokshaws. In addition to weaving, the men were renowned for being growers of flowers. Most of the weavers sold their goods in Paisley, the main centre for weaving. This meant the Pollokshaws weavers had to transport their goods by horse, but when the Glasgow to Paisley Canal opened in 1810 many of them took their cloth to Dumbreck and travelled by barge to Paisley, making the journey much quicker.

According to the Post Office Directory of 1899/1900, R.G. Gourley, upholstery and cabinet maker, was at 1118 Pollokshaws Road, at the corner of Moss-side Road and Pollokshaws Road. Both properties in the picture appear to belong to R.G. Gourley, with advertising hoardings stating 'House Jobbing Done', 'Carpets Lifted, Cleaned and Laid' and 'Window Blinds Repaired'. The buildings were demolished when the site was needed for Shawlands United Free Church (later the parish church) in 1901.

Introduced in 1750, tolls were intended to pay for the upkeep of the roads and were paid at toll bars to a toll keeper who would have lived in a nearby house. On the road to Glasgow, Shawlands Toll (seen here) was at 'High' Shawlands, at the junction of Pollokshaws Road and Shawhill Road, just past the location of Shawlands Primary School today.

Samuel Dow Ltd was established in 1807 when Samuel McCalman Dow came from Lochaber and opened a bar at 45 King Street in Glasgow. As the company grew, it was known for its range of blended Scotch whiskies and a number of public houses in Glasgow. Samuel Dow, the grandson of the founder, developed the business further. In 1881 a bar was opened at 226 Great Western Road and the company headquarters moved to 242 Clyde Street from Mitchell Street. In 1899 a public house was opened at 1157–1159 Pollokshaws Road (seen here). In 1931 another bar was opened at 67–71 Nithsdale Street in Pollokshaws. The Samuel Dow public houses are now under the control of Ind Coope (Scotland), a subsidiary of Allied Breweries.

Now housing Shawlands Primary School, Shawlands Academy on Pollokshaws Road was built in 1893 and designed by the firm James Hamilton & Son. This was one of James Hamilton's last projects before his death in 1894. He and his son John worked on it together after a year of disagreement between them. John employed his own son, Arthur, to design additions to the school between 1899 and 1905. In 1930 Thomas Baird designed a much bigger building on Moss-side Road and it opened as the new Shawlands Academy secondary school in 1933.

Boys and girls from Shawlands Academy performing in a Pageant Tableaux in Langside Halls in April 1907. This photograph shows Queen Bess and her court. Langside Halls was originally the National Bank of Scotland at 57 Queen Street in Glasgow. It was designed by John Gibson and opened in 1847. When Mount Florida, Langside and Shawlands became part of Glasgow in 1891, the council had to provide a public hall for the area. It was decided that the bank building was suitable and so it was dismantled and rebuilt in 1901 under the supervision of the City Engineer A.B. McDonald. The halls continue to be used for a wide variety of concerts, community functions and activities.

The church with the stained glass gable windows behind the tram was Shawlands Parish Church, designed by J.A. Campbell of Burnet, Son and Campbell. He began the designs in 1885 and the building opened in 1889. In 1893 the hall and session house were added. It began as Shawlands Mission or Preaching Station. In 1929 it changed its name to Shawlands Old Parish Church. In 1963 Langside Avenue Church united with it and then in 1998 the congregations of Shawlands Old and Shawlands Cross (originally the United Free church) joined to become Shawlands Parish Church. The building is constructed of light coloured Giffnock stone. The gable looking toward the picture was based on Dunblane Cathedral and the three stained glass windows were completed in 1950 as a war memorial by Douglas Hamilton, a renowned artist in stained glass. The church building is now used by the Destiny Church.

The top picture is a view through the railings of Shawlands Parish Church and Shawlands Cross across Moss Lane. The front of R.G. Gourley's property can be seen on page 21. The picture beneath is the view from the other side, probably from what is now Frankfort Street looking towards the church. All these buildings (apart from the church) have been demolished.

In this photograph there is a wine merchant at each corner of Minard Road at Pollokshaws Road. The window on the right advertises Dunville's VR Old Irish Whiskey. It was a rare pot still whiskey distilled by Dunville & Co at the Royal Irish Distillery in Belfast. It was introduced in 1837 and discontinued in 1936. In the 19th century various temperance societies started up in an attempt to combat the social evil of drunkenness, and in the Pollokshaws area there were a number of such societies including the Total Abstinence Society, the Order of Good Templars, the Pollokshaws Temperance Society, the Order of Rechabites, the Sons of Temperance and the British Women's Temperance Association. It is likely that the machine going down Minard Road was built by Aveling and Porter, a British company that was the most prolific manufacturer of steam road rollers in the world.

This 19th century picture at Westfield Lane shows the last remaining part of old Westfield (Crossmyloof) at the corner of Minard Road and Pollokshaws Road. Minard Road runs down at the right hand side of the tree with the stone at the base. The shop at the left was owned by Peter Campbell, a grocer and wine merchant. He must have prospered, as he had a telephone, the number of which was 56 Langside. The property next door belonged to George Muir, a slater.

Towards the end of Minard Road, the entrance to Crossmyloof Station can be seen at the far right of the photograph. The building is no longer there: all that can be seen now is a concrete wall with stairs leading down to the station. The photograph must have been taken on a warm day, as almost every flat has its windows open. The tenants of these flats paid on average £22 per annum in 1913/14. Some of the tenements in Minard Road had additional names, suffixed by 'Terrace'. For example, one block is named Darnley Terrace and was numbered differently from its numbers today.

Minard Road is first mentioned in the 1893/94 Post Office Directory. The undeveloped land to the west of Pollokshaws Road was known as the 'Lands of Westfield'. Part of the area was in use for orchards and nurseries. Some of the land was available for speculative investment and advertisements were published in 1883. According to the advertisements, part of the attraction of the land was that it was within 'a short distance' of Strathbungo Station. This was because Crossmyloof Station was not opened until 1888, but Strathbungo had been opened in 1877.

On the left of the photograph is the Waverley Cinema in Moss-side Road. Owned by Shawlands Picture House Limited, it opened as the Waverley Picture House on 25 December 1922 and seated 1,320. In 1928 a Christie 2 manual theatre organ was installed. The cinema was taken over in September 1929 by Associated British Cinemas and the organ was removed from the building in 1953. It was renamed the ABC in 1964 and was a cinema until 1973. Later it became a bingo hall, then a snooker club in 1982. By 2002 it had become derelict before being sold to the G1 Group and used as a nightclub and bar. The church on the right is the back of Shawlands Parish Church.

Waverley Gardens, like Springhill Gardens, were a typical Victorian feature designed to serve the residents of the tenements adjacent to them and to add to the attractiveness of the buildings. The tenements were built around 1901 and were owned by various groups of trustees, who then let them to tenants. Rent varied between 17/- per annum to 27/- per annum depending on the size of the flat. The tenants were mostly employed as clerks, travellers, bookkeepers and salesmen. The 'Glasgow Style' can be seen on the canted windows.

Dinmont Road in Shawlands is part of the Waverley Park development, a residential area to the east of Shawlands Station. It is bounded by the Cathcart Railway line, the Glasgow–Kilmarnock Railway line, Pollokshaws Road and Moss-side Road. The opening of Shawlands Station in 1894 saw the beginning of house building in the area, most of which was completed by 1907. The area is noted for its common building height and streets laid out in a grid pattern. It comprises mainly of residential properties: short terraces and semi-detached villas. The architecture of most of the buildings is a basic Arts and Crafts style. Almost all of Dinmont Road was owned by George Eadie who lived in Hampden Park Villa in Mount Florida. His business in Mathieson Street is listed as a brick builders, valuators (property), mason, builder, wright and timber merchant. Rents on Dinmont Road varied from £21–£40 per annum in 1905/06.

Photographed in 1951, these villas are in Pollokshaws Road, near Ravenswood Drive (part of the Waverley Park development).

L.M.S. Crossmyloof.

The train company that originally owned this line was the Glasgow, Barrhead and Kilmarnock Joint Railway, founded in 1848. Their trains originally ran from Southside Station, a Caledonian Railway passenger terminal situated at the junction of Cathcart Road and Pollokshaws Road at Gushetfaulds in the Gorbals. When that station closed in 1879, the trains ran from St Enoch. Crossmyloof Station opened on 1 June 1888 some ten years after Strathbungo Station, indicating that Strathbungo was a much more densely populated area at the time. The overline station building seen here was removed in the late 1990s and the overbridge at Titwood Road was rebuilt in 2006.

Tenement buildings such as these in Springhill Gardens replaced older individual buildings along Pollokshaws Road. Springhill Gardens were built on the site of Springhill House which had been the home of Henry Murphy, a pawnbroker and hat manufacturer in the Bridgegate. Later the house became Springhill Academy. The tenements were built in 1904 from a design by Glasgow architect John Nisbet. The flats vary in size and the gardens are surrounded by the 'U' shaped block.

Old Strathbungo Village was just inside the Parish of Govan. The old name for Strathbungo was 'Marchtown' and there is still a March Street in the area. The village grew as a place for crofters and miners when Sir John Stirling Maxwell of Nether Pollok began to feu out land around Titwood. By the end of the 18th century weaving had become the mainstay of the 35 families living there. John Houston, a weaver from Paisley, introduced weaving to Strathbungo and 80 weavers worked in the village for his son William who had set up a manufacturing business. Tenement building began in the area in the 1870s. The first church, a chapel of ease, was built in 1838 and a church was erected two years later. Strathbungo's first school began at the start of the 19th century, but by 1840 it had a permanent building in March Street. Strathbungo Public School opened in 1894. The building is now St Bride's Primary. The other school, at the north end, was Cuthbertson Primary, opened in 1906.

These buildings were part of the village of Potterfield in Haggs Road. The site of the village can be seen through the railings of Pollok Estate. It was situated between Shawmoss Road and the junction with St Andrews Drive. Although not part of Shawlands and Newlands, these images do give an idea of what the area would have looked like in the 19th century.

This cottage was probably in Shawlands or Newlands, but it is impossible to say exactly where.

Marlborough House was designed by architects Whyte and Nicol, and built between 1915 and 1920. It was commissioned by William Kerr, a chef and entrepreneur who had made his name by running a tearoom at the 1911 International Exhibition in Glasgow. The Marlborough became his flagship restaurant. However, he was not a generous employer and was infamous for the low wages he paid to his staff. Waitresses were paid twelve shillings per week for a twelve-hour day and were fined two shillings if they broke a wine glass and 9d for a cup. The Marlborough was later bought over by A.F. Reid and Sons. The function suites were named after battlefields where the Duke of Marlborough led his troops to victory in the 1700s: Oudenarde, Malplaquet, Ramillies and Blenheim. When rock 'n roll arrived in the 1950s it became the 'in' place to be as a dance hall. It was bought over in 1968 by Reo Stakis, but shortly after that it was almost destroyed in a fire before being redeveloped as a club. In the early 1970s Glasgow comedian Billy Connelly performed there in the 3rd City String Band for a fee of £75. It is now named The Shed and owned by Glasgow entrepreneur Michele Pagliocca. The bar at the end was known as the Corona Bar. It was built in 1912–13 by Clark & Bell for James O'Malley. Above the entrance door to the bar is a small plaster hand with a cross superimposed on the palm, said to symbolise the name of Crossmyloof. The name may have come from a number of sources, one of which has a connection to Mary, Queen of Scots. Allegedly, before the Battle of Langside she declared 'by the cross in my loof (palm) I will overcome my enemies.' It is also said that she stated 'by the cross in my loof I will be there tonight in spite of you traitors' when she was warned that escape was impossible. However, many historians believe that the name has nothing to do with Mary, Queen of Scots, but may be derived from the Gaelic *Crois MoLiubha* or St Malieu's Cross (although there is no clear reason recorded as to why this may be). It is also possible that it is a compound of Latin and Gaelic in connection with a cross of elm wood with which it was customary in Catholic communities to mark the boundary of a parish.

South Shawlands Church, at the corner of Deanston Drive and Regwood Street, opened on 9 May 1913. It was originally South Shawlands United Free Church and the first minister was the Rev. William Muir. In common with many Glasgow churches, the halls opened first in 1909 until funds could be raised to build the church. Miller and Black, a Glasgow firm well known for church design, were the architects. The church is now within a linked charge with Shawlands Church of Scotland at Shawlands Cross.

This photograph shows Stevenson Drive (now Deanston Drive), with Skirving Street on the left. Further along Stevenson Drive was Crossmyloof Public School, opened in 1877 by Cathcart School Board. The building was converted into flats in the summer of 1996. On 7 April 1941, during a German bombing raid, a single large bomb and a few incendiaries fell on the corner of Deanston Drive and James Grey Street. No. 33 Deanston Drive completely collapsed, and numbers 31 and 35 were badly hit. A total of eighteen people died in the incident and ten people were trapped in a shelter in Afton Street.

Tantallon Road and Langside School, Shawlands.

After the Education (Scotland) Act of 1872 many schools were established in Glasgow under the auspices of the Glasgow School Board which existed from 1874 to 1918. Langside School, designed by Andrew Balfour and constructed from pink sandstone, opened on Tantallon Road in 1904. For a time, Langside Primary used Crossmyloof Public School (opened in 1879) in Deanston Drive. Tantallon Road was formerly called Albert Road; when various burghs became part of Glasgow some of the streets were renamed to ensure that there weren't duplicates. The road originally had a number of villas along the same side as the school with names such as Endrick, Belize, Durley Dene and Mo Dhachaidh, and some of these still stand.

This picture of Walton Street was taken from the corner of Albert Road (now Tantallon Road) looking up towards Kilmarnock Road. The buildings in the distance are some of those that were demolished to make way for the Shawlands Arcade. Rent was between 18/- and 27/- per annum and all the flats were tenanted. They were occupied by salesmen, cashiers, clerks, grocers, travellers and others with similar jobs.

*Left:* The Langside Monument at the top of Langside Drive commemorates the Battle of Langside which took place on 13 May 1568. The actual battle took place where the Victoria Infirmary now stands. Eleven days after she escaped from Loch Leven Castle, Mary, Queen of Scots had drawn together an army of 6,000 men. The Earl of Moray, the regent of James IV and Mary's opponent, brought his troops, numbering 4,000, to the hill that is now Queen's Park. Her army was defeated: approximately 400 men were killed within 45 minutes. The monument is made of granite and was erected in 1887. It was designed by Alexander Skirving, after whom Skirving Street was named. The sculptures are of a lion with a cannonball under its paw and the column is decorated with thistles, roses and fleur-de-lys as seen on Mary, Queen of Scots' coat of arms.

*Above:* Algie Street was named after the Glasgow tea and coffee merchant Matthew Algie. The old village of Langside was centred on the street. By the 18th century there were approximately 20 cottages and the 1841 census shows that most of the residents were cotton handloom weavers. By 1861 there were only six weavers left. The weavers also cultivated fruit and flowers. As tenement buildings became more prolific in the 1880s, the village disappeared, although some of the weavers' cottages were still there in 1905.

Tramcar 822 was brought into service in 1900 and scrapped in October 1950. The parked van advertises James Craig's tearooms at 14–34 Kilmarnock Road. Behind the tramcar on the left-hand side and further along Kilmarnock Road was the Embassy Cinema, owned by Harry Winocour. It was opened in February 1936 by Harry Lauder and the first film screened was *Casino de Paris* with Ruby Keeler and Al Jolson. The cinema was designed by James McKissock to seat 1,638 patrons and it had a stage and dressing rooms. In 1938 it was sold to the Glasgow Photo Playhouse Company, but in 1968 it was demolished to make way for a supermarket that was part of the Shawlands Arcade. The balustrade along the top of the shops at the left has gone, but the building remains essentially the same.

KILMARNOCK ROAD, SHAWLANDS

Some of the villas seen here on Kilmarnock Road were Westfield House, Rose Cottage, East Shaw Villa, Westfield and Firbank Cottage. Tramcar 830 would have been travelling towards the Pollokshaws Depot, which was later replaced by Newlands Depot in Newlandsfield Road. After 1935 this tram moved to Springburn (Possilpark) Depot. In the 1930s many of the retail units on Kilmarnock Road, starting at Shawlands Cross, were given modernist fascias and contemporary interiors. Good quality materials were used to give the shops an 'upmarket' feel and many of the shop fronts were finished in black vitrolite with chrome shop name lettering.

Carment Drive (on the right of the picture), off Kilmarnock Road, was named after the solicitor of the last Laird of Pollok. James Hamilton, the architect, lived at No. 22. He also designed a number of monuments in the Necropolis, including those of John Henry Alexander (an actor-manager), David Robertson (a prominent bookseller) and the Aikens of Dalmoak Mausoleum (John Aiken was a wealthy Glasgow wine and spirit merchant). The railway bridge over the road leads to Pollokshaws East Station, part of the Cathcart Circle. The station was built on a bridge high over the River Cart. The Cathcart District Railway Line via Queen's Park and Crosshill got as far as Cathcart on 25 May 1886 and the circular route back to Central Station in Glasgow via Pollokshaws and Shawlands was completed on 2 April 1894.

Strictly speaking, Grantly Gardens was in Pollokshaws. The address probably got its name from Lord Grantly, a son by a previous husband of the second wife of a Laird of Pollok. The spelling of the name Grantly changed to Grantley, possibly when Pollokshaws was annexed to Glasgow in 1912. Street names were changed to avoid confusion with ones that existed in Glasgow at that time. The message on the back of this postcard is rather poignant. The card was dated 18 February 1919 and the sender has written, 'Arrived home this morning, once more a civilian which is a blessing'.

The Hub Cycle Company can be seen here at No. 268 Kilmarnock Road. The cycle shop has a bicycle sporting four saddles; this may have been used as an advertising device. The other two bicycles belong to Munro Butcher's, next door at No. 270. The cycle shop advertised that it was the official repairer to the CTC, the national cycling charity which championed the cause of cycling. Alex Munro was a large chain of butcher shops with branches all over Scotland. However, by 1995 there were only thirteen shops left trading under that name, although the company had previously been bought over by J.H. Dewhurst, a large butcher chain that traded outwith Scotland. Dewhurst was part of the Vesey Empire which specialised in meat imported from South America, mainly Argentina.

Macquisten Bridge spans the parish boundary line between Eastwood to the north and Cathcart to the south. There had been a road from Pollokshaws to Giffnock which, having crossed the Cart, ended up at what became Nellie's Toll, now Eastwood Toll in Giffnock. It was replaced in the 1830s by a new road from around the area of Shawlands Cross. This meant that a new bridge, Macquisten Bridge, had to be built. Designed by Peter Macquisten, a Pollokshaws civil engineer, it was constructed around 1832. The parapets and edges of the arch barrel are granite and the rest of the structure is red sandstone.

This view of Auldhouse Road at Riverford Road has changed very little, apart from cars being parked all along the street. It is possible that the name Auldhouse has its roots in two Celtic words – 'ald' meaning a burn and 'hus' meaning ghost or spirit. It is also possible, of course, that it merely means 'old house'!

This picture was taken from near Langside (Newlands) Station looking towards old Millbrae Bridge. Millbrae relates to two mills on the banks of the White Cart Water – a paper mill and a corn mill. Neither building survives today. Newlands Station in Tannahill Road was on the Cathcart Circle Line. It opened as Langside in 1894 and was renamed Langside and Newlands on October 1901. It was renamed Langside in 1962. In 1966 the original station burnt down, but a modern one replaced it.

This photograph was captioned 'Flooding at Millbrae Bridge January 1932'. Millbrae Bridge crosses the White Cart on Langside Drive. It has had a variety of names: White Cart Water Bridge, Cathcart Old Bridge, Netherlee Road Bridge and Old Snuff Mill Bridge. The bridge was part of the Gorbals to Carmunnock Turnpike Road and the original bridge had a stone marked 1624 on it. That stone was incorporated into the present 18th century bridge. Until the 1890s most of the area around the bridge was open countryside, with bluebell woods and formal gardens at Langside House near Camphill Avenue. In 1991 questions were asked in the UK Parliament with regarding to the flooding of the River Cart and a modern flood prevention scheme was eventually started.

Construction of the villas in Earlspark Avenue began in the early 1900s and Bronze Age cinerary urns were discovered on the site in 1904. The urns are now in the Royal Museum of Scotland in Edinburgh. They contained cremated human remains. A bright green stain was found in one of the urns and it is believed to have been caused by a bronze object, possibly a razor. An alternative name for the nearby White Cart water was the River Earl. The name was in honour of Earl Cathcart, but was never really adopted. However, the name continues in the name of the avenue. The title Earl Cathcart was created in 1814 for William Cathcart. He was a descendent from Lord Cathcart who was raised to the Peerage of Scotland between 1447 and 1460. His descendents also fought at the Battle of Langside in 1568. The family seat is Gateley Hall in Norfolk.

The street on the left is Newlands Road and the railway bridge on the right is on Langside Drive. The house at the top of Corrour Road, in the centre, is Tower Brae. It is still there, although massive trees now block the view of the house. Just out of sight on the left is Dairsie House School, part of The Glasgow Academy. Dairsie House was founded in 1900, originally using premises in Monreith Road under the name of Cathcart and Newlands Private School. The name changed to Dairsie House in 1919 when it moved to its location in Newlands Road.

MERRYLEE ROAD, NEWLANDS

Merrylee Road runs from Kilmarnock Road to Clarkston Road and is mainly a residential area of substantial Victorian villas with large gardens. By 1907 the building boom in this area had virtually ceased and few villas were built after that. Owners' (not tenants') occupations listed in the valuation rolls were as varied as coal agent, slater, linen manufacturer, writer, undertaker, electrician and ship broker among others. Further along the road is Merrylea Holy Trinity Parish Church, built between 1912 and 1915 in Romanesque style and designed by P. McGregor Chalmers. The church is built of Auchenheath stone on ground gifted by Sir John Stirling Maxwell of Nether Pollok.

This picture shows Nellie's Toll, now Eastwood Toll. In 1882/83 the Kilmarnock Turnpike Road opened and tolls were collected here. It is believed that the toll was originally named after one of the toll keepers.